The Nativit...

FOR KIDS AGES 3-8

MW01504055

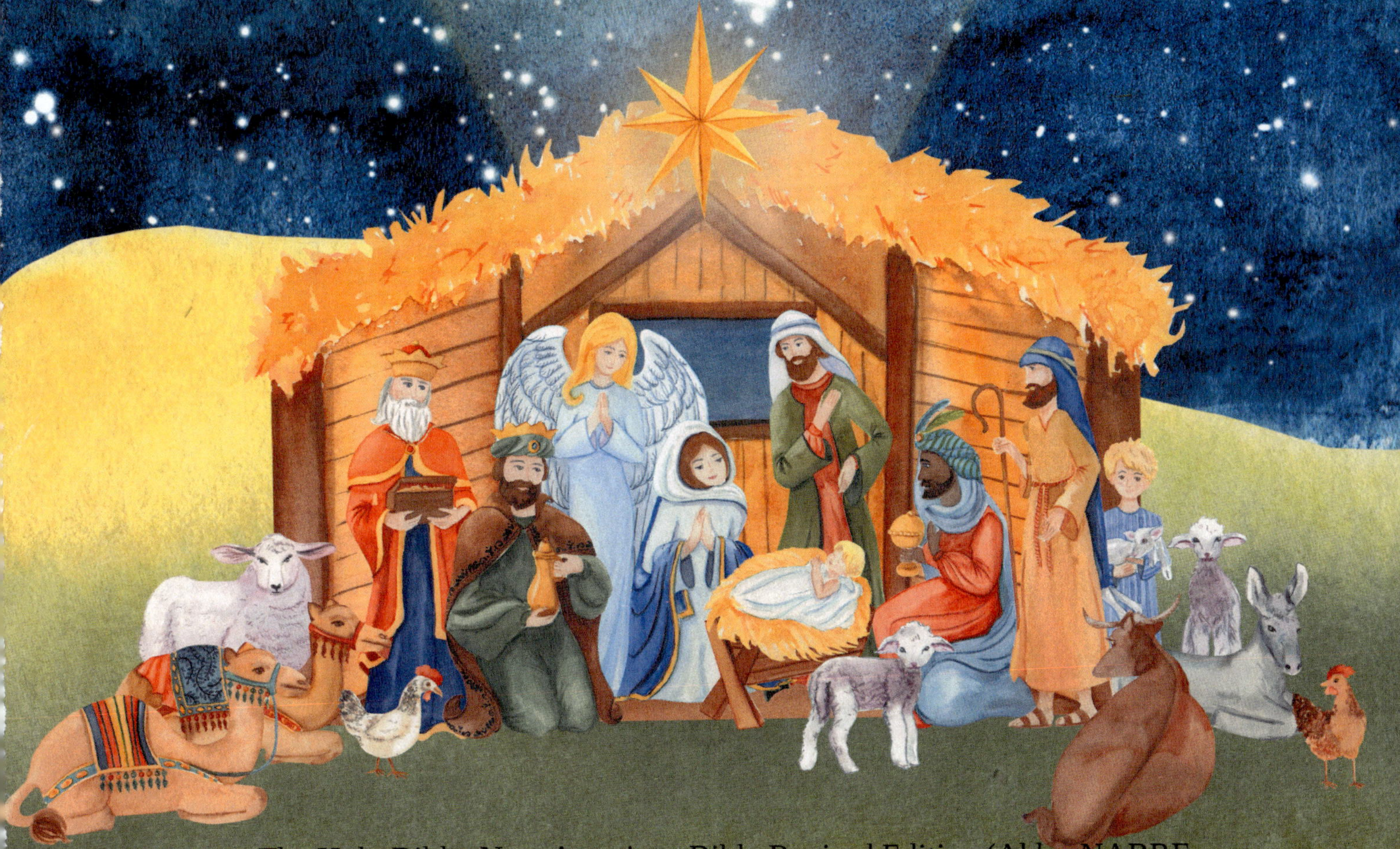

A Gift for:

....

From:

....

Date:

....

4

Christmas is coming! But did you ever wonder why we celebrate Christmas? The Christmas story, when we remember and celebrate Jesus' birth in Bethlehem around 2000 years ago, is the most important part of Christmas for us.

The Christmas story begins in a town called Nazareth. A lovely young lady named Mary lived in this town. She helped others and was loved by everyone. Mary was engaged to Joseph, a good and honest man.

The Story in the Bible:
Luke 1:26-38, Matthew 1:18-24
Luke 2:1-20, Matthew 2:1-13

The angel Gabriel was sent from God to a town called Nazareth to Mary. And coming to her, he said, "Hail, favored one! The Lord is with you. Do not be afraid, Mary, for you have found favor with God. You will bear a son, and you shall name him Jesus. He will be great and called the Son of the Most High."

"The Holy Spirit will come upon you, and the power of the Most High will overshadow you. Therefore, the child to be born will be called holy, the Son of God." Mary said, "Behold, I am the handmaid of the Lord. May it be done to me according to your word."

Part 1. The Annunciation
The Visitation - Luke 1:26-33
Mary's Obedience to God - Luke 1:34-38

8

The angel of the Lord appeared to Joseph in a dream and said, "Joseph, son of David, do not be afraid to take Mary, your wife, into your home. For it is through the Holy Spirit that this child has been conceived in her. She will bear a son, and you are to name him Jesus."

When Joseph awoke, he did as the Lord's angel had instructed and welcomed his wife into his home.

Part 2. Joseph's Dream
Joseph's Dream - Matthew 1:18-24

In those days, a decree went out that the whole world should be enrolled. So all went to be enrolled, each to his own town.

And Joseph too went up from the town of Nazareth to the city of David, which is called Bethlehem because he was of the house and family of David, to be enrolled with Mary, his betrothed wife, who was with child.

Part 3. Birth of Jesus and Shepherds
Travel to Bethlehem - Luke 2:1-5

11

While they were there, the time came for her to have her child, and she gave birth to her firstborn son. She wrapped him in swaddling clothes and laid him in a manger because there was no room for them in the inn.

Jesus Christ, the Savior of the world, was born that night.

Part 3. Birth of Jesus and Shepherds
Mary, Joseph, and Jesus - Luke 2:6-7

13

Now there were shepherds in that region, living in the fields and keeping the night watch over their flock. The angel appeared to them, and the glory of the Lord shone around them.

The angel said to them, "Do not be afraid; I proclaim to you good news of great joy. For today in the city of David, a savior has been born for you who is the Messiah and Lord. And this will be a sign for you: you will find a baby wrapped in swaddling clothes and lying in a manger."

And suddenly there was a multitude of angels, praising God and saying: "Glory to God in the highest, and on earth peace to those on whom his favor rests."

Part 3. Birth of Jesus and Shepherds
The Angel and Shepherds - Luke 2:8-14

15

When the angels went away from them to heaven, the shepherds went in haste and found Mary and Joseph. And there was the baby, lying in the manger. When they saw this, they made known the message that had been told them about this child. All who heard it were amazed. And Mary kept all these things in her heart.

Part 3. Birth of Jesus and Shepherds
The Visit of the Shepherds - Luke 2:15-20

When Jesus was born in Bethlehem of Judea, in the days of King Herod, magi from the east arrived in Jerusalem, saying, "Where is the newborn king of the Jews? For we saw His star in the east and have come to worship Him." When King Herod heard this, he was greatly troubled. Then Herod sent the magi to Bethlehem and said, "Go and search diligently for the child. When you have found him, bring me word, that I too may go and do him homage."

Part 4. The Visit of the Magi
King Herod and the Magi - Matthew 2:1-8

19

After their audience with the king, they set out. And behold, the star that they had seen at its rising preceded them until it came and stopped over the place where the child was. And on entering the house, they saw the child with Mary, his mother. They prostrated themselves and did him homage. Then they opened their treasures and offered him gifts of gold, frankincense, and myrrh. And having been warned in a dream not to return to Herod, they departed for their country by another way.

Part 4. The Visit of the Magi
The Visit of the Magi - Matthew 2:9-12

When they had departed, the angel of the Lord appeared to Joseph in a dream and said, "Rise, take the child and his mother, flee to Egypt, and stay there. Herod is going to search for the child."

After King Herod died, they came back to Nazareth, and Jesus grew to be filled with grace, wisdom, and kindness

EGYPT

23

Merry Christmas!

The Nativity story reminds us that, no matter how simple or humble our beginnings may be, there is a spark of divinity within each of us. It teaches us to embrace kindness, generosity, and the spirit of giving. Just as the wise men brought gifts to the baby Jesus, we too can share our love and kindness with those around us.

We'd appreciate it if you could take a few minutes to leave us a review.

Thank you for reading our books!

We work for you, so please help us follow the right direction through feedback, reviews, and suggestions.

Made in the USA
Las Vegas, NV
19 December 2023

83175930R00017